Her Brightness In the Darkness

A Memoir of
Tragedy, Hope and Triumph

By Lois Sack

Her Brightness in the Darkness
A Memoir

Copyright © 2010 by Lois Sack

All rights reserved.

This book was written by Lois Sack speaking for her deceased daughter, Jody Lynn Sack. All the anecdotes and vignettes are true but they are written in a first person voice by a second person and therefore the choice of words may vary slightly.

ISBN 1449555403
Printed in the United States of America, 2010

The Lamplighter

She has taken her bright candle and is gone

Into another room I cannot find

But anyone can tell where she has been

By all the little lights she leaves behind

--Author Unknown

Dedicated To

Jody's many friends in Philadelphia, Atlanta, New York and anywhere they have landed; and her dad, Ben, and her brother, T.J, who believed in her abilities and were right.

Foreword

The vignettes in this book are all true. The book was written by me, Lois Sack, through the inspiration of my deceased daughter, Jody Lynn Sack. I heard all the anecdotes before she died. She communicates with me by helping me remember the many funny and sad things she experienced. I do not know from what level or sphere her voice comes, I only know she moves me along.

Table of Contents

Chapter		Page
1	Whatever Will Be, Will Be	1
2	Hope, Hope Squandered	4
3	A Second Chance	6
4	To See or Not to See	8
5	Family and Friends	13
6	You Can't Always Get What You Want	15
7	The Old Me	22
8	The Rocky Path to Recovery	24
9	My Coach	28
10	A Rough Start	31
11	Throwing Something Back	35
12	Oh Friendship	38
13	Brightness in the Darkness	42
14	A Race for Breath	48
15	Summer Jobs	51
16	Bigger than Life	52
17	Jobs and Journalism	55
18	J'adore Paris	57
19	Marathon Girl	61
20	Away Down South in Dixie	64
21	Just Do It	68
22	I Love New York!	71
23	One Fatal Misstep	79
Newspaper Quotes		84
Addendum: Eulogy by T. J. Sack		85

Chapter 1   Whatever Will Be, Will Be

I slipped and fell four stories to my death at age 25. I knew as I was falling that my mom, when she learned of my fall, would cry out, "Oh Jody girl, I told you to be more careful." She was always telling me to be careful, ever since I was two and I fell out of the grocery store basket, and when I fell down the barn ladder hitting every rung with my face, and when I ate all of my father's pack of NoDoz, and when I ate my grandmother's roach poison, and when I split my foot on the fireplace mantel while doing cart wheels, and when I flipped my car when I was 17.

My life was a series of accidents. I guess I had the attitude of "if it happens, it happens" as part of my biological make up. I feared little. I would just do what I wanted and figure whatever is meant to be is meant to be.

I was living in New York City when the final accident happened. People who knew me would always say, "Jody, do you think you should live in New York?" I knew what they meant but I pretended I didn't and would say, "Why not?" They would say, "But aren't you afraid?" and I would answer, "Of what?" The reason my friends and family worried about me is that I was legally blind since that accident when I flipped my car when I was 17. That was my second-to-worst accident.

    The car accident knocked me out for hours. The paramedics had to cut my hair to get me out from under the car. When I was examined in the emergency room, they determined that I had a serious head injury. I also had a collapsed lung, endocrinology malfunctions, some bad cuts, possible spinal cord damage, and I don't remember what else. They induced a coma so that I would keep perfectly still.

    My mom says she warned me when I went out the rainy night of the accident. She said, "Use your seat belt. Don't drive so fast. Watch out, it's slippery." Then she says she knew something bad was going to happen to me that night. I was "distracted," she said. She claimed I was in a daze much of the time. Well, I had a lot on my mind. It was August and I was going to leave in a week to start at University of Virginia. I was going early because I was going to play lacrosse and the team was going to have fall practice. I wasn't afraid, but I was nervous. I guess I was a little spacey. I was told that the police determined that I had been driving too fast, I skidded on the slick surface, hit a stump next to the curb, the driver's side car door opened and I was partly outside when the car landed on me. I wasn't wearing a seat belt and I had been drinking. I was 17 and I never listened to my mom's constant warnings.

Chapter 2   Hope, Hope Squandered

Recovery from a serious head injury is a humbling experience. The doctors said to my parents, "If she lives, we just don't know how she'll come out of this. She could be a very different person. She could have a different personality. There is a good chance she'll never be able to go to college. She may not get back her former intelligence. She may be blind. Don't expect too much." When I awoke from my induced coma, I heard a little of this but I didn't care about most of it. What's to be, will be. I just wanted to see better. I was almost totally blind.

About a week after my accident, my friend Christie Barber came to visit with a balloon that said, "Get Well Soon." I saw the balloon and surprisingly read the writing. She also brought me an audio tape with greetings from some of my friends. I was so happy. I told my parents about reading the words and they were happy. The doctors were a little skeptical, except for my favorite resident, who believed me. Unfortunately, it was his night off. During the night, the pressure built up in my head to such an extent that the doctors had to put in a shunt. The next day was a rough one for my mother. She came to see me with her friend, Sue Foulke, who knew a little about medicine and could translate "doctor language" for my mom. They watched the numbers on machines that indicated pressure in my head. The doctors said the high pressure was not good for my brain or my vision. My father was called at work to come quickly to the hospital. The doctors said I might die any minute.

Chapter 3   A Second Chance

I didn't die that day. I like to say, "God gave me another eight years." And, once I got over the car accident, I made the most of my short visit to this planet.

I stayed at Pennsylvania Medical Hospital for a month. Most of my physical problems were "improved." I had received excellent medical care, especially from my favorite resident who, in addition to being a resident in neurology, was a boxer. I learned that he was supposed to box in the 1980 Olympics but couldn't go when the USA backed out because we were in a cold war with the Soviet Union. Instead, he was going to the next Olympics as the neurologist for the boxing team.

I was his favorite patient and he was my favorite doctor. He had saved my life in the emergency room, for which I was grateful, but he had also cut off most of my long, blonde hair, which was devastating. He said it was thick with blood. I never did see the reasoning for cutting it because of blood but I forgave him. Once, when we were talking about the high school we had both attended, he admitted that he had had a crush on one of my favorite teachers. In September, when school was back in session, when one of my high school friends was visiting me at the hospital, I couldn't resist asking my friends to tell the teacher that one of her former students was my doctor. Wouldn't you know, she visited me a day or so later. After the visit, she told me she was going to the cafeteria for a snack. I quickly got in touch with the resident and they "met" again. I think both of them loved hearing from each other how "special" they were. I am sure my resident confessed having a crush. I am also sure that our teacher, being an upstanding professional, would not have encouraged him but she must have been flattered.

Chapter 4 To See or Not to See

The docs at the hospital had done all they could for me. I was beginning to wear out my welcome when I kept falling out of bed thinking I could walk. I left in an ambulance to start my rehabilitation at Bryn Mawr Rehabilitation. When I arrived, I was put into the locked-in head trauma unit. My mom was ticked off and told the head nurse that I did not belong there. She thought the other patients were mentally deranged and I was "almost" normal. She was reassured that I was in the right place. They pointed out that, because of my head injury, my thinking was slow and fuzzy; I was still unable to walk; I could not hold my head up while sitting in a wheel chair; I couldn't feed myself; and my speech was slurred. I also had some endocrine dysfunction and was taking medicine that might cause seizures. And I was almost totally blind.

  I didn't mind the head trauma unit at all. The people were interesting. My visitors, the young ones, liked a patient nicknamed, "The Tour Guide." In his wheel chair, this head-injury patient greeted all visitors to the head trauma unit with the offer of a tour. He gave a good tour, taking people from door to door telling them who "lived" inside and at least a brief of description about them. There were certain doors that did not open without a key. The Tour Guide would ask the visitors to get the key at the desk and bring it back to him. His ploy to use the key in order to escape never worked, but he kept on trying.

I take credit for helping my roommate speak, even though what she said made me angry. She'd had a severe stroke and there was worry that she would never speak again. Then one morning, after I had been told not to try to get out of bed, I decided I was going to get to the bathroom by myself. I rolled out of my bed and crawled to the bathroom, went, and began to crawl back. As I exited the bathroom on my hands and knees, my roommate said, "Bad girl." I was afraid she would tell the nurse so I said, "Shhhh." Then I realized she had spoken and I said, "That's great that you talked." She said, "You're a very bad girl." I couldn't get back into the bed and got a lecture from the nurse.

During my three months at Bryn Mawr Rehab, I took two breaks for experimental eye treatments. The first was at The University of Vermont School of Medicine for surgery. Dr. Robert Sofferman explained the surgery as lifting bone fragment off my optic nerve, kind of like lifting a fallen branch off my leg so that my leg could function again. He could do this without cutting my scalp, but by inserting instruments through my sinuses at the back of my mouth. I was so excited. My mom told me we would be driving by mountains on the way and it would be a beautiful drive. Maybe I could see the mountains on the way home. I had no doubt that this blindness ordeal was temporary and I would soon be seeing 20/20.

The ride to Vermont was fun. My mom's friend, Carolee Norton, went with us. I met my doctor and he was so nice. During the MRI, I laughed and was feeling silly. I was not nervous about the surgery. My mom and Carolee and, back home, my dad and brother, were very nervous. They knew it could backfire and I could lose the little bit of sight I had. The surgery took about six hours. When I woke up, I was all set to yell, "I can see, I can see!" But, I couldn't see at all. Dr. Sofferman said it would take several days before the blood around my eyes cleared up. I got to know my roommate who was legally blind. It seemed, to me, like she could see fine. There was also a minister there who was legally blind. He said his biggest problem was tripping on the little floor signs that say "Wet floor."

The next few days I was nervous. I wasn't seeing any better. In fact, it was probably a month before I saw somewhat better. I didn't get to see the mountains on the way home. That was one of the biggest disappointments of my life. However, I do think the surgery helped in the long run. For several months I saw some improvement, but nothing dramatic.

    The next experiment was at the University of Pennsylvania School of Medicine. The doctors there said steroid treatments might help. I tried for a week but my sight did not improve. I was back at Bryn Mawr Rehab in just about the same condition as I started.

    I worked hard at Bryn Mawr Rehab. They gave me physical therapy, occupational therapy, psychotherapy, and the finest in personal care. After a month, I was moved from the head trauma locked-in unit to a more advanced unit. I missed Pattie, who had been my favorite nurse, but I made up my mind to adjust.

    My psychologist, Dr. Barry Jacobs, wrote a chapter in a book about me. He wrote that I was like he was as a youth. We had one personality for parents and teachers and another for our friends. We worked hard to please our parents, but we had no regard for "the rules" when with our friends.

    My parents later learned that when I was in high school I went to a bar in Philadelphia that served minors, drank, and drove my friends home. What was I thinking? Probably, "Whatever will be, will be."

When I was working diligently in rehab, I was mentally OK. But when I was awake and had no appointments, I was bored and scared and lonely. Being scared and suffering consequences was new to me and I did not handle it well. I called my parents at work and begged my mother to come be with me. But in the early evening hours I usually had visitors and that was fun. Two old boyfriends came, and one, Jimmy Riley, crawled into bed with me and we talked. We were both silly and, for a few minutes, I forgot all my problems.

Chapter 5   Family and Friends

I was home in time for Thanksgiving. Our family does holidays with Carolee Norton (my mom's friend who went to Vermont with us) and her two daughters, Kelly (my age) and Holly, three years younger. When we three girls and my brother (ranged from six to thirteen years old) got together, we had so much fun in the Norton basement practicing songs and routines which we presented to our parents. When John Norton (Carolee's husband) was alive, he always made sure my brother, T.J. (four years younger than I—everyone's "little bro") got his share of time in the video of the "concert." Usually T.J. would be the guitar player, or the announcer, while we three girls were the famous singer/dancers. Those tapes, shot by Carolee's sister's husband, are precious, because John died a year after my fall and seeing him on tape makes the families feel his energy. His final five years, he lived in a nursing home in Honeybrook, Pennsylvania. What a great nursing home it is. On holidays, when John was there, the Nortons and the four Sacks would arrive at Honeybrook with everything we needed for a Thanksgiving or Christmas dinner. We would finish the cooking there and eat in a room that could be reserved for families like ours. Often, other "guests" were invited, like Carolee's sister Linda and my cousin Mary Sack who was a student at Brown University. Mary usually had one or two friends with her. Also, neighbors of the Nortons, and residents of the home, would drop in.

We found many things to laugh about at these holiday dinners. For instance, there was the time our dog (a large cock-a-poo named Rollie) came with us and suddenly was missing from the festivities. He was going deaf, so we couldn't whistle or call him. Next door to our large "party" room, some singers were serenading a group of residents with Christmas carols. There was Rollie, lying down between the audience and the singers, obviously enjoying whatever sounds he heard. We had a hard time getting Rollie's attention and getting him to come back to our room.

Another funny incident happened at the nursing home, in John's room, during a regular, non-holiday visit, a year after I had gotten out of rehab, I saw, on the wall next to his bed, a very large picture of me standing and looking straight ahead. I knew John liked me like a niece, but I didn't think I rated such a large photograph and where did he get it? At first, I pretended I didn't notice it, and then I finally began staring at it and the picture moved. I almost yelled "The picture is moving," when I realized I was looking in a mirror. By this time I was getting to love it when my blindness created a laugh.

Chapter 6 "You can't always get what you want but you try, try, try and you will find...you get what you need."

--The Rolling Stones

With my base now at home, I was allowed to do my rehab at a commercial rehab center close by. I was back in my room, sleeping in my bed, lying on our couch with my faithful dog, Rollie. That part was great. But, after the initial flood of visits from friends, I became very lonely and depressed.

About visitors. The ones I enjoyed came to see me because it made them feel good cheering me up. They were there to see me, to kid around with me, to laugh at their stories or my stories, or to take me for a walk in my wheel chair or on foot. But there were a few groups of parents with their children who obviously wanted their kids to see what happens when you do not obey the rules. I could almost hear them saying when they got home: "See how crippled she is—that can happen to you. Use your seat belt. Do not drink and drive."

Being alone most of the time made me appreciate my old life so much. I had it all. I was smart enough. I was good-looking enough. I was athletic enough. I had enough friends. I had kind enough parents. And I had blown it. My life was changed forever. I felt sorry for myself. I was close to suicidal. I wrote this note:

"I am so confused. I don't know how to deal with this visual impairment. I hate it so much. All I think about twenty-four hours a day, seven days a week is my stupid injury. Sometimes I wonder if it's worth living. I can see a little bit, but it's not enough. If it doesn't get any better, I'll feel like my life is not worth going through the hassle of living. I know that is an awful thing to say, but I haven't thought of any other solutions. I think, personally, that committing suicide sounds like a big cop-out, but that's the old me. The old me was and is all that I ever want to be. The old me was fun-loving and carefree. The old me was interesting and talkative. The new me, in a word, sucks. I am just a bump on a log. I am no longer fun and exciting. I am boring and lifeless. I sit around all day and watch TV or listen to talking books. Now what kind of fun is that? The crazy thing is that I have no desire to do fun things. I am scared. That would never have happened to me before my accident.

The only reason, at this point, that I am saving my life is because of my mother and father. They love me so much and they couldn't bear to see me die. I have no idea why they love me so much, because all I am to them is a hassle. But I love them so much and I couldn't stand to break their hearts.

I sincerely hope I get in another car accident, because I don't think it will be easy for me to go on living. It will also make it a lot easier for the people around me."

People who have never felt suicidal probably don't understand it. It's a hopeless feeling. It's when you can't see the way to improvement in your life. I didn't recognize that I had already improved immensely. Through rehab and just time, I was now walking almost normally, I had regained most of my balance, I had regained strength in my arms; I was talking almost normally; I was able to smile (kind of a side-smile smirk); and my hair was growing back (very important). I was becoming proficient at using the computer (thanks to special lessons through the Pennsylvania Association for the Blind), I had learned tips on getting around (through instructions on the

cane method of walking); and I had ventured out with my dog Rollie for some walks in the neighborhood, although I refused to use the cane because I was not ready to be a spectacle, create pity in strangers seeing me, or admit that I was so blind I needed a cane.
After promising my parents that I would not kill myself, slowly but surely, I began to hope again. The three things that turned me from desperate to daring were having a loving family and some good, good friends, doing well with the two courses I took at Villanova University, and running and working out. Not as important to me, but important to my mother, was some plastic surgery to my collapsed cheek bone and eye muscle surgery so that my blind eye traveled in the same direction as my partially seeing eye (prior to surgery it tended to go up to the top of my socket). The improvement in my appearance put people at ease and they forgot about my being different. Fortunately I guess, prior to the facial surgery, I wasn't seeing well enough to notice the bizarre look of my eye drifting up. I was aware though that most every other 17-or 18-year- old girl had long hair and mine was still too short!
    The loving care from my parents and younger brother was constant. I could depend on them to be a comfort and to guide me in the right direction. Rollie was also a tremendous comfort, lying at my feet on

the sofa while I watched TV or listened to my talking books. A strange accident took place during this period. Rollie was hit by a car. He was injured in his hip. The veterinarian said we could let nature take its course and let it heal by itself or do surgery which may help. We opted to let it heal on its own. Rollie and I became kindred spirits, limping about the house and going on short walks.

    I should also mention my fabulous younger brother, T.J. His life changed as mine did after my accident. He now had a blind sister. Everyone felt bad for him. He became a sort of solemn celebrity. We grew up fighting all the time until the spring before the accident. I had always considered him a pest, wanting his fair share of TV programs, his spying on me (my imagination), and just existing. Then in the spring of my senior year in high school and his last year in middle school, I noticed that he was way cooler than I ever was at his age. He was on every team possible as a starter or captain; girls thought he was really cute; and he had a high I.Q. I began to appreciate him and he became a great friend. I confided in him. To this day I could bet anything that he still keeps the secrets we shared. Later, when I moved to Atlanta, he came to visit and it was so much fun. My friend, Anna, and I visited him at College of Charleston and he actually seemed proud of me. It touched me deeply. When a brother can be a great friend, there is hope for both that love can be eternal.

Most of my friends were away in college. I had been recruited by University of Virginia to play lacrosse, something I had worked hard for in high school. I had been so excited about the adventure of going to college and playing lacrosse, which had been the plan the summer before my accident. Anticipating playing on a championship team was gone, but going to UVA was still my goal.

A few of my friends opted to stay near home for college. The two that were the greatest source of re-establishing my independence and love of life were K.C. Waldron and Kate Gibson. Some people are more caring than others. These two friends included me in their parties, movies (I could see part of the movie screen from the 20 percent of sight I had in my left eye), and just going out for a Slurpee at the local 7-11 shop. K.C. and Kate always made me feel good, at least halfway intelligent, and not too ugly. When Kate arrived at my house to pick me up, she would always greet me with, "Jody, I love your hair." I would answer, "I love yours." My father had a good laugh imitating us. I don't know how I could have recovered socially without my two good buddies. When my other friends came home from college, several called on me. My friend Jen Vare must have been born with empathy. She always knew how much to help me and how much to leave me alone while walking or at parties or bars. When she was home, we always had fun and we even got in a little trouble. But that's another story!

I think good friends are precious gifts. Loyalty could be the 11th Commandment. I wonder how I would have been if one of my best friends suddenly became crippled, less attractive, blind, and less witty and amusing. I believe that one should make friends for life, and as with marriage, stay friends through the bad times as well as the good times.

Chapter 7   The Old Me

When I say all I want is to be the old me, I'm asking a lot. That does not mean I was perfect or even very good. But, I was motivated and goal oriented. From the time I was a freshman, I wanted to be the captain of the lacrosse team at Radnor High School. To the players, being captain was proof of skills and popularity. Senior year, when I was elected co-captain, along with the outstanding player Patty Parishy, it was one of the nicest things that ever happened to me. It was important to me so I was conscientious about my responsibilities which included planning dinners at my house and Patty's house to charge up the team.

The old me set a record for running at Radnor Middle School and a record for best time for a girl in the biathlon (swimming and running) at the high school. My back stroke record at Conestoga Swim Club still stands. The old me was a member of the National Honor Society. All my achievements were built on my goals. I was also able to help other people through the service clubs I belonged to including the Surey Club (for seniors) and Trevor's Campaign for feeding the homeless. Now, I am the one who needs help!

Sometimes, but not very often, I remember some things about the old me that I do not like: lying to my parents and drinking and driving for instance. My mom says I am sweeter and kinder and have more empathy since becoming blind. As I understand it, Buddhists believe kindness creates happiness. So, why wasn't I happy?

Chapter 8   The Rocky Path to Recovery

At the new year, 1991, I took two classes at Villanova University which is conveniently situated practically across the street (Route 30, Lancaster Avenue) from my house. My subjects were The History of Ireland and Western Civilization. I checked with University of Virginia to be sure these courses were transferable. I hoped and dreamed of going to UVA (one year later than scheduled) in September if I could master these two subjects.

It turned out that the academics were, for me, the easiest part of going to college. The hardest part was trying to appear normal. I did not want people to know I was blind.

My right eye was totally blind and I had 20 percent of vision in my left eye. I could see words on a page, but reading was slow because my eye had to search for the next line and/or paragraph. I had a hard time with a blackboard because I couldn't see the whole thing, but only parts of it. While a professor was talking, I could take notes but I had not regained my former small motor control and my handwriting was messy and sometimes I could not read my notes. I was always thinking "Am I conducting myself normally?" I would imitate other students. I forced myself to laugh and even to say something, clever.

The good part was I soon learned that, intellectually, I was not only almost back to normal, I was considered smart! My mom should have gotten credit for my classes, too. In the beginning, she read to me almost every evening. Sometimes I would fall asleep while she was reading and she was so involved in the book she would just keep on going. I also received tremendous help from Talking Books. This nonprofit organization has a library of books on tape, which they supply free to anyone with a visual disability or dyslexia. If the organization does not have the book the student needs, they will record it within a few days. They sent me tapes to play on my big yellow tape player supplied by the Pennsylvania Association for the Blind. Another helpful benefit for visually-impaired people is that the U.S. Post Office will ship material for "the blind" free of charge. When I finished a talking book, I would turn the label around and mail it back to the headquarters in New Jersey. Sometimes I felt guilty having a book especially recorded for me and then only "reading" a small part of it. I consoled myself by thinking, "Someday if I am rich, I will donate a bundle of money to them."

    The hard part of going to college for me was the loneliness. I was not boarding at Villanova so I had no roommate to pal around with. I did not belong to any clubs or after school activities. I was so busy trying to look normal that I probably seemed preoccupied. I could not make eye contact with a person speaking until I located the person who was speaking. On campus, when passing someone from my classes, I could not see face and hands at the same time so I could not see people waving hello or smiling at me. I did not make one friend at Villanova! I realize now that it would have been better if I had told people that I was blind. Then, if they saw me on campus I might not see them, so they should yell to me instead. My troubles were compounded by a lack of coordination (dizziness, messy handwriting) which interfered with my walking (I looked tipsy or drunk).

 One bright exception in the "I don't have any friends at Villanova" complaint was having an occasional lunch with someone I knew before we were students at Villanova. Kevin Sousa and I had been lifeguards together at Overbrook Country Club, while I was in high school. I had helped him get his job. I had worked there three summers and we both really liked working with the kids on the swim team (I had been on the swim team in high school and had grown up spending my summers at Conestoga Swim Club where I was a contender in the back stroke). Kevin was really cute and friendly and sweet and caring. But I had known him from my "life before the accident." What guy in his right mind would like me if he just met me now? I felt doomed to a single life.

Getting to and from my classes took almost 100 percent of my concentration. At that time, there was no "walk" light at the place where I had to cross Lancaster Avenue (a heavily traveled route). I tried to see the traffic light or I just followed other students. One time, I waited and waited, through two green lights, for a student to cross, only to discover that it was a pole, not a student I was waiting for. It got so, in the following seven years of my life, that my stories of things that happened to me because of my blindness became part of my personality. I laughed hard at myself, and my friends laughed with me. You could call it "Brightness (sparks of fun) in the Darkness."

When I first received my schedule at Villanova, my mom and I went to the campus and looked for the buildings and then the classrooms. We then walked from the house to the campus to the buildings to the classrooms several times so that I was familiar with the route. We also walked to the library, student union building, cafeteria, and bathrooms. All went well during the semester until I was detoured to another building where I had to take a test. At the entrance were seven steps. I fell down all of them. I was horrified. I cannot remember feeling any pain from the fall, just the humiliation of not being normal.

Chapter 9   My Coach

    I actually have some advice to offer. If you are down and out, if you are disabled in some way, if you feel inadequate, then exercise. It helped me probably more than anything else. I was lucky to have an amazing coach, who pushed me, encouraged me, and gave me precious time. It was my father. Dad is an exercise nut and a golf fanatic. But more than that, he loves to teach and help people.

    When I came home from Bryn Mawr Rehab in November, he would go for walks with Rollie and me. He picked up the pace little by little. Soon, by late December, I ran a few steps. Because of my head injury, I was off balance and my coordination was poor. While in the hospital I had developed "foot drop," and that may have been a reason for my right foot to drag and cause me to trip, walking and running. I had been a cross country runner in high school and I imagined and prayed that I could run like that again.

    In the winter, dad and I and sometimes my mom would try a little running at the basketball pavilion at Villanova or at our exercise club, La Maison. One day, Mr. Bob Kelly, a friend of my parents and the father of my brother's good friend, Mike, got us invited to meet the Eagles football team.

I was a football fan and very excited to meet the coach and players. I had my picture taken with their quarterback, Randall Cunningham. But something even more exciting happened. I ran for a distance across the parking lot with my father, brother, Mike and Mr. Kelly. It was then that I knew I would someday, once again, be a runner.

I did not always think running was so great. One time, while running at our exercise club, my dad and I were planning to do our usual two miles. After falling three times, I decided I would quit. I burst out to my dad, "That's it, I quit." Usually, he said, "No, you're not quitting," but this time he said, "Okay, let's leave." "What?" I yelled. "You know you won't let me quit. Why are you saying that?" We started running again and I was angry. I didn't trip anymore that day. My dad says I'm "feisty."

But running wasn't all I did to regain my strength and coordination. I lifted weights and worked out on the strength-building machines at the exercise club. I got a job at the club the summer after the semester at Villanova, mostly as a sitter for toddlers whose parents were working out. But sometimes I would get other assignments, including polishing fixtures and weight machines. One day a handsome sports caster, Lou Tilley, saw me spraying the air instead of a mirror. He kidded me about it and

I quibbled, "The air needs cleaning, too." He realized I had very limited vision and from then on, we were friends. Years later, when I had a copy writing internship in New York, I often called him for his opinion of the copy or campaign I was proposing.

Chapter 10   A Rough Start

I got A's in my two courses at Villanova. I was determined to go to the college that had originally accepted me, the University of Virginia (rated as the #1 state university at the time in "Newsweek"). I know I surprised a few people who thought I would not regain my intellect. I was even able to think abstractly, which I could not do right after the accident. I was very, very lucky. One of my friends from high school, Ann Tauffen, who was one year behind me and had been a partner in crime in several high school incidents, was going to Virginia also and had asked me to be her roommate. In addition to being smart and athletic and pretty, she was a caring person who I think wanted to help me make my way. I was pretty nervous about going to UVA, but knowing Ann and Maggie Kelly (also from Radnor) and some others, helped me to feel more secure about going off to a college so far away from home.

I still considered myself an athlete. I had even considered going out for track and field. Then I heard that there was a crew team for women at UVA. I mentioned this to Ann and we both decided to take rowing lessons on the Schuylkill River (Philadelphia) the summer before going to UVA. We learned on singles, rowing up and down Boat House Row with the boat attached by rope to the pier. Encouraged, we decided to try to walk on to the team at UVA.

    My parents and I went to UVA a week before the other freshmen arrived. We stayed at a golf club through the membership of my parents' friends, the Suplees. It seemed quite luxurious and my dad could hit balls at the range so he was happy. The week went well. We practiced walking around the campus, with me trying to remember where the stairs were, where there was a dangerous area next to the sidewalk, and of course how to get from one place to another. I was excited and optimistic. Little did I know it would be the year from Hell.

    The day the other freshmen arrived and my parents left was ok until they actually said "goodbye." I walked them to the edge of the quad where my dorm was located. With great bravado, I kissed them and then, after all that practice, walked towards the wrong dorm. They saw this but kept on going. My mom says the ride home to Pennsylvania was the worst ride she has ever taken. She cried all the way. Me, I was embarrassed and confused, but sadness did not hit me until a few days later. Everything was new and exciting and scary. I had a great roommate. I had made it to the college of my dreams. Then, a few days later, everyone in our dorm went to a football game except me and I was left totally alone. It wasn't that people didn't like me; it was just that freshmen have to look out for themselves and be aggressive in making friends and this was difficult to do with me pretending I was normal, not blind, but acting a bit off beat. If only I had started out telling everyone I was legally blind. I know if I had explained my situation, it would have made my life a lot less traumatic.

Then there was crew. As a freshman, I was, according to my coach Kevin Sauer, the worst member of the team (he told me this later). He probably felt sorry for me and let me stay. Then, I had to take two busses to get there, by myself. Eventually, one of the members who had a car offered me a ride back and forth. Also eventually, my coach noticed something that changed his mind about my future. He saw that I was a good runner, fast and determined. I had no choice of sports, if I was going to be an athlete, it had to be crew. When rowing in an eight person boat, all you have to see are the hands on the oar in front of you and, with my limited vision, I was able to focus on those hands. You do what those hands do. One of the great things about crew was you are either rowing or working out and, boy, did we work out! I was in a light-weight boat and therefore watched my weight. I was 5'8" and I kept my weight at 128. Crew training was the best thing I could have done for my continuing rehabilitation.

Ann Tauffen, my roommate, was one of the best first-year rowers; and I was dead worst. But, being at the bottom, I made friends with others who were struggling. Thank goodness for the crew friends I made because they were some of my only friends that first year.

Chapter 11 Throwing Something Back

> *"I've learned that you shouldn't go through life with a catcher's mitt on both hands. You need to be able to throw something back"*
>
> --Maya Angelou

Fortunately, my first year at Virginia, I had the opportunity to meet some of the most caring and admirable faculty and "special" student helpers. Through the four years, I learned from people who loved teaching and some who actually knew the poets and other writers we learned about and read. One of my professors was Julian Bond, who was a famous civil rights advocate, and he had known the Reverend Martin Luther King. He told us some wonderful stories about Dr. King

Intellectually, I tried to read as much as I could. It was very slow because my good eye could only see a word or so at a time and I often lost my place going from line to line down the page. I was much better with Talking Books. Thank goodness when I was home I had a computer and had taken a couple lessons from an instructor employed by the Pennsylvania Association for the Blind. My papers were not too hard to produce and I received good marks

Most wonderful of anything I had ever experienced before in school was the office where anyone with a physical or learning problem goes to get the help they need. UVA made sure I had books recorded for me, either by Recording for the Blind in Princeton, NJ, or by volunteers at UVA. Some of my (later) friends volunteered and spent hours reading the text books, etc. out loud so that I could listen to the assignments on tape through a talking book machine.

I was one of a few blind students who visited the office frequently. Also visiting were deaf students, students with learning disabilities, and students with physical disabilities. Some of us who received help from the office also volunteered to help some of the other students. One assignment for me was to take a quadriplegic boy, Dan, from his room to one of his classes. I had to enter his room, help him put on his jacket if needed, and push his wheel chair to his class. For this class, he used an old fashioned wheel chair instead of his electric one, because the classroom doorways were not wide enough for the electric chair. Once we got to his class, I would help him take off his jacket and make sure his tape recorder was turned on. All went well until one day I was running a little late. When we got to the long hallway before his classroom, he said, "Run, Jody, I'm going to be late." I did as he said and ran. We were both laughing when we ran smack into a boy turning a corner. I had not strapped Dan in and he went flying out of his wheelchair. As the boy that ran into us was helping me put Dan back in his chair, he said to me, "What, are you blind?" I answered him, "Yes, what are you, stupid?" He just said, "Holy S…!"

Chapter 12   Oh, Friendship

My second year at Virginia was sooooo much better. The main reason was that I was invited to join a sorority. Boy, did I worry about getting into one. "Rush" was nerve racking and fun at the same time. I got to meet many really nice girls, and Alpha Chi Omega turned out to be great for me. I pledged it because of one girl, really, Amy Stanton, who took an interest in me and said she admired my spirit and courage. Other people have said this to me, but I could tell Amy really meant it. Years later, she became a veterinarian. I would say her animal patients are pretty lucky.

My sorority house was on the grounds (at UVA the campus is called the grounds), on the quad where many of the other sorority and fraternity houses are situated. It was easy to find my way around in that area and there was always activity in the quad, including inter-fraternity and inter-sorority games.

I am happy to say I was never lonely at UVA again. My sisters were caring, helpful, and most of all we had fun together. They listened to my stories about my mishaps and we always ended up laughing. Karen Prise, my roommate for two years, was good at imitating me. She would say, "This is Jody, every night: 'Where is my psychology note book. I looked everywhere. Karen, you must have it. SOMEBODY STOLE MY NOTEBOOK.' Then she would find it in the most obvious place."

Well, then there is my love life. I had dates, all right, but most guys did not ask me out a second time. One or two dates with me and they seemed to be scared off by my clumsiness. Knocking into people at a bar, sticking my hand in someone's drink, talking to the wrong person (thinking he or she was someone else) made most guys insecure or embarrassed. All the guys that is except Matt Gully. He is a really good-looking guy, fun loving and athletic. He showed me new areas of the grounds, went running with me, and treated me as "normal." We kissed and made out but somehow or other we became friends more than boyfriend, girlfriend. He was one of the few boys I met who could laugh at my crazy incidents and not get scared when he was a part of them. A couple years after graduation, when I was living in Atlanta and my brother was going to college in Charleston, S.C., Matt decided he would run with me in Charleston's big five-mile run, which went over the famous Cooper River Bridge and continued beyond into Charleston. He knew I would fall a couple times because he had run with me before. But he had no idea how often I would cut people off and literally ram into them. After the race, as I was getting my knees bandaged in the first aid tent, Matt said, "You didn't tell me I was going to be running guard and telling people 'excuse us' every minute!" He said we got some dirty looks. Then we laughed.

Another time Matt and I, during our summer vacation, decided to participate in a Philadelphia team triathlon. He would swim (he was a high school swimmer who kept up with it), Ann Taufen (my roommate first year at UVA and a friend in high school) would ride her bike, and I would run. Matt came to my house (he lived in Richmond, Virginia) the night before because we were going to have an early start. We went to pick up Ann, and she was just putting her bike together. She seemed pretty relaxed about it but already Matt and I were nervous about the time. We arrived just in time for Matt to get in the water (I had pre-registered). The water was the Schuylkill River, probably one of the dirtiest rivers in this country. His father had told him he was crazy to swim in the Schuylkill. While rounding a bend, Matt's arm swung and hit a row boat being mismanaged by a volunteer official. In the crash, Matt swallowed some of the river. Boy did he pay for that—sick for a week. Meanwhile, I was next with running. I got off to a flying (literally) start running smack into a skate boarder who was not supposed to be on the path we were to follow. I bled all the way to the end. Finally,

Ann did her part. She rode that mountain bike with all her heart and soul. Unfortunately, everyone else had racing bikes with gears for everything. Ann did get encouragement from the residents of Philadelphia though—"Go, you girl on the mountain bike!" We did not come in last, which was a great surprise. I count that day as one of my fondest memories with Matt and Ann. After I died, both married and had beautiful children. They both talk to me and "yes," I try to answer but you are not always listening. Oh, by the way, Matt, thanks for being a pallbearer at my burial (even though you were late and everyone had to wait for you). Duh!

Chapter 13 Brightness in the Darkness

I entered several running races while at UVA. I might have won one of them for my sorority except the organizers had designed a new place for the finish and I went the wrong way and tripped over a curb. My knees were bleeding and everyone started yelling at me, but when I finally got straightened out, I finished third. I and some of my friends who were there found that telling the other sorority girls about the incident was actually more fun than winning. Thank goodness they found humor instead of sympathy—they knew that's the way I wanted it.

Another funny incident was when my crew coach, Kevin Sauer, was trying to rally the team for a meet, he said, "I want you guys to row as hard as you possibly can. I want you to row yourselves blind." I retorted, "Ha, ha, ha coach, I already did that." Coach Sauer apologized but most of the crew did not hear him over the laughter.

My sorority roommate, Karen Prise, loves to tell stories about me, even now (I'm listening, Karen). She considers it ironic that I made English Literature my major when so much reading is involved, and so many papers have to be written. One of Karen's favorite stories is about me misplacing things. As I mentioned earlier, Karen says I was always losing something. Inevitably, every morning a paper was due. After staying up late, I would wake up at 5 a.m. for crew practice and gather things I would need for the day. "Oh, God! Oh, God! It's gone!" would echo through the walls of our second floor room. While I repeated, 'It's gone! It's definitely gone!' with terror in my voice, Susan (our other roommate) and Karen would take note whose turn it was to get up and find the paper. One of them would get up and look in one of two spots where the lost items usually were: my desk or on the floor next to my bed, always finding them within a few seconds. They would hand me the paper, and send me on my way.

    Karen also got a few chuckles about the way I read all those millions of books for English. I found the best way to read was by listening to a talking book recording and follow along in the printed book as best I could. When you get used to the talking book machine, you can make it run faster than anyone would normally talk. Karen tells it this way: "Jody would listen to some books at Mach 1 speed. I was convinced she was listening to Chipmunks Greatest Hits."

    But there were a few books that I could not get recorded and because I did not have the machine on to block out noise, I became very distracted. One time when I couldn't seem to concentrate with all the noise of a sorority house, Karen offered me her extra pair of rubber earplugs. She handed me one and waited for me to get it in and ask her for another. But instead she heard me say, "Oh, no! Karen, can you help me?" I had ripped the earplug in half and used one half for each ear. Well, the one in my left ear was stuck. With the help of our friend Ann Wray, we tried to get it out with tweezers, but we were unsuccessful. So, off to UVA hospital we went. Even though Karen was studying to be a nurse, she had a hard time explaining to the triage nurse what I had done. The earplug was so far into my ear that my balance was affected and I tipped over when I stood up. Fortunately, the staff at UVA hospital got it out and no damage was done.

My parents dreaded my 21st birthday. They had heard too many stories of the trouble celebrants got into at colleges, like drinking 21 shots and dying of alcohol poisoning. That afternoon, by telephone, my mom said to me, "Don't end up in the hospital tonight. I don't want any calls at midnight." Karen tells the story of that night best: "We had just had a huge snow storm during the week. It left a sheet of ice covering the streets and walkways of Charlottesville. We made it through the whole evening, 9 p.m. to 3 a.m., going from bar to bar on "The Corner" and Jody did not fall or even trip once. On our way back up the back steps to the sorority house, as Jody was bragging about this accomplishment, she slipped and split her chin open. As usual, Jody laughed since she found the irony much more amusing than the pain of a split open cut on the chin. Once again, off to the hospital we went for stitches."

    Granted, I was accident prone and blind, so I was bound to have mishaps. Add to that, I had more accidents than most because I was in a daze much of the time. I concentrated more than I should on looking normal (not blind). I guess it is true what people told me, I was still somewhat fearless although not as fearless as I used to be.

    My mom was in shock one time when she was visiting the campus. We were about to cross the street at the edge of the campus, along a pedestrian crossway (stripes of white) and I didn't hesitate going across. She said, "Jody, don't you look before you walk? I answered, "Well, if I get, hit, it's the driver's fault, this is a pedestrian crossway and we have the right of way."

    A final incident at UVA involved a phenomenon of the Eighties, but it was actually a tradition at UVA for many years before that. It is streaking. At night, one would sometimes see running, nude bodies streaking across the commons (the lawn at the center of the grounds). From one end to the other it is about 100 yards. It is recommended that every student do this before he or she graduates. Let's just say, most do not do it and they do just fine in life. But, always looking for adventure, I did it with a group, one at a time. Unable to see much, especially at a distance, I was unaware that there was a small audience at the end, checking us out. I'm glad I didn't know until it was over!

UVA was a great experience for me. It gave me confidence for the rest of my life. I ended up with a high grade-point average and friends I still talk to but maybe they don't hear me. Maybe they do.

Of great surprise to many of the crew team, my fourth year at UVA, I ended up with the sixth seat in the No.1 lightweight eight. Every position on this boat, except the coxswain, has to earn the seat through numerous in-team competitions so there was no way anyone could say Coach Sauer "gave" me the seat. I think he was more surprised than anyone. We got the bronze in the international championships (1995) in Worcester, Massachusetts, one of the most prestigious collegiate crew races. We were all so happy and I was the happiest of all.

A year after I died, Kevin Sauer and Tom Allen, a "friend" of the UVA women's and men's crew, and the members of the crew teams assembled in October and christened a brand, new, totally awesome boat to be used by the No. 1 team for women's eights. It was black and exciting looking compared to the older, white boats. They christened it the "Jody Lynn Sack"

I was there in spirit, listening to Coach Sauer's dedication. He had always been there for me, through the very bad to the very good. Under his coaching leadership, I had gone from the worst (first year) to one of the lucky ones chosen to row in the first lightweight eight (fourth year). I had also been awarded the "Teamwork Award," by a vote of my teammates.

My brother represented the family at the christening. His acknowledgment speech brought tears to some of those present and certainly to me. He talked about how hard I struggled to get to UVA and how being on the team was so important to me, and how crew had helped me so much, both physically and mentally.

T.J., your words were so kind, you must have forgiven me for the time I took from our parents while you still needed them. The tears I shed at the christening were the good kind.

Did anyone notice the mist on the river?

Chapter 14   A Race for Breath

The reason my parents missed the christening of the "Jody Lynn Sack" boat was that they were running in The Radnor Run. The run had been going on for almost 20 years and benefits the American Lung Association of Pennsylvania. Some friends and neighbors, including Bob Main, Dick Jackman, John Chobert, and others had written to the committee asking them to name the race for me, in memory of my determination and other reasons I can't say with any modesty. Well, the committee did the next best thing and began awarding a Jody Lynn Sack cup to the fastest female runner. The first year after I died, a bunch of my friends and neighbors attended and some of the most surprising people ran the five miles over some pretty serious hills. Others ran and some walked a one-mile race. Now, years later, it is fun for me to watch the group that shows up every year including my brother, TJ, his wife, Lauren; Karen McFadden, and sometimes her children and grand children; my cousin Mary and an assortment of her friends coming from New York City; the three Nortons (Carolee, Kelly, and Holly); Kathleen and Howard Weiz; *Main Line Times* Sports Writer Bruce Adams; Vicki Thompson, Kathleen and Andy Thompson, and, one year, their kids Brian and Amy; my aunt and uncle

Kringy and Alexander Gordon-Watson (strictly as observers); Scott Miller and his wife, Kate, Sue Suplee; Susan Clotsky, Jan and Bob Main and the Strongs (Pat, Dick, and their three sons). To the many other friends I did not mention, thanks for participating.

A hot addition to this group is Lou Tilley, the sportscaster and columnist I met while dusting the air at our athletic club, La Maison. He is my friend forever. He promoted the race on his CN8 Sports TV show and in his column in *The Main Line Times*. Then he comes to the race and announces the winners. He still likes me and I still like him. I also like his gorgeous wife Diane who is a beautiful runner and person. During the Radnor Run, instead of trying for a medal in the 5-mile run, Diane runs with her young daughter Katie O'Connor, who at age 10, ran a 7-minute mile.

The race has grown in popularity and now attracts about 800 runners and walkers. I notice more of my parents' friends are there, which pleases them immensely. My mom is even on the committee. My old friends are more likely to call on me for advice and courage than show up at the race. Either way is wonderful. But, I must warn my contemporaries who call me for advice and think I'm their guardian angel—look out. I wasn't too adept at guarding myself. You can trust me with emotional stuff, but please don't trust me with your bodies. You know what I mean!

Chapter 15   Summer Jobs

Summer jobs, when you are in college, are usually a way of appreciating college because the jobs are so bad. However, I liked my summer jobs because they made me feel normal and productive. Although my parents paid college tuition and board, I needed a job for my spending money. You might think it is hard to get a job when you are blind. Well, let's say I networked. My first college vacation summer job was "life guarding" at Overbrook Golf Club, a carry-over from my high school summer jobs. It did not work out—I was assigned to the baby pool where all the mothers watched their children anyway. I felt stupid and resigned. It was nice of management to put me on the payroll, but I knew then that you can't look back; you really have to look ahead.

My friend Karen Elitsky worked as a telemarketer and she got me an interview. I memorized the script and was able to get the job and finish the summer trying to convince office managers that they needed my company's newsletter. I did OK, but Karen was the star. She was a born salesperson. I was never able to hang up on a telemarketer after that.

Chapter 16 Bigger than Life

This first college summer was shortened work-wise because my family decided to take a very special summer vacation. My mom chose it mainly because she felt I needed to get a particular area of my confidence back. The area was mobility. It was her version of an Outward Bound vacation where people go into the woods and survive on what they find. Our trip was quite a bit more fun than that. We rafted down the Colorado River, halfway through the Grand Canyon, and then climbed to the top.

I must admit I was scared, but no more scared than everyone else. Being in crew at UVA, I was at ease with the paddling and not afraid of water. But approaching the rapids was awesome. It was the roar, getting louder and louder. The guides told us to keep paddling hard, don't stop. Fortunately, none of us tipped over. At one of the rapids, the guides said we could get out of the boat and ride the rapids. About half of us did, including me, T.J., and my dad. We had to keep out feet ahead of us, lying on our backs. Of course we wore life jackets. It was so scary. You have no control. You are totally at the mercy of the river. It is amazing that as cold as the water was, about 50 degrees compared to the air, which was about 100 degrees, none of us mentioned being cold. That was the least of our worries.

    I was sad when we left the group that was going all the way down the river to the end of the Grand Canyon, but we had signed up for seven days and then to climb up the North Rim of the canyon. The guides said to me, "Don't worry. It's like walking up a street." Boy, were they wrong. It was by far the most difficult thing I ever did. The trail started off as wide as a sidewalk, not too steep. Then it got more and more and more narrow. But the worst part is, it was rocky, with big rocks jutting out of the path. With only limited vision in one eye, I was unable to see ahead and the path at the same time. My father and mother took turns saying, step right, step left, big rock coming up on your right. It was grueling doing that all the way (one mile high, but nine miles in getting there because of winding around) while carrying 40-pound backpacks and ascending a steep trail. I can remember stopping at two rest stops. At the first one, T.J. decided to strike out on his own. He couldn't stand going at our pace. It took us seven hours.

    At one point, my Mom stopped and said, "Wow, look at that view. It's awesome!" I kept saying, "Where, where?" and my dad, who is afraid of heights, said, "No way, I'm not going to look." My mom was the only one who really saw the Canyon at its best.

Chapter 17   Jobs and Journalism

Another summer job while I was in college was an internship at the brokerage house, Solomon, Smith Barney, located near home. I called people whose names appeared on list after list. If I could interest them in considering investing through Smith Barney, I would check them off and my dad, a stockbroker there, would call them back. In addition to learning about the stocks business, I made a very good friend—Margaret Dexter. She and Lisa, another broker's assistant, were lots of fun to be around. Margaret and I and her fiance, Mike Hussey, and Lisa had several adventures together, after work of course. Margaret, thanks for being such a good friend.

My most interesting summer job was working as an intern for WCAU-TV, at that time the NBC affiliate in Philadelphia. I worked for Herb Denenberg, a lawyer consumer advocate. Everyone in Philadelphia knew who Dr. Denenberg was, some liked him and some thought he was a total nerd. But there was not a single intern who did not love him. He treated us like special students and we learned so much about TV and advocacy.

Wanting all the "journalistic" experience I could get, I took a part-time job at a local weekly paper, *The Suburban and Wayne Times*, wrapping papers, inserting ad books, and other physical duties far removed from journalism. However, that summer of '93, I had other plans. More about that later.

My other true journalist summer job was working as an inside writer for the *Philadelphia Inquirer*, Neighbors section. I did some court reporting and features and quite a bit of telephone research for the editors and reporters.

Chapter 18   J'adore Paris

I went to Paris for two weeks with my mom, during the summer of 1993. Visiting Paris had been a dream of hers since she was a girl. I, too, wanted very much to visit Europe. Visiting Paris was a great place to start.

Poor Mom. She studied her French for a year before we left. She listened to tapes while she ran, studied at home for hours at a time, and announced to me that we will do well in Paris because she would be able to communicate. Well, at the beginning of the flight from Philadelphia to Paris the flight attendant spoke in French and I looked at my mother to see if she was getting it. I saw a blank expression. She turned to me and said, "I didn't understand anything." We were doomed.

But we were sooo lucky to be staying in the 16 Arondisement, close to the Arc de Triomphe. We took a bus and then a cab to the entrance to the high rise. My mom was friends with a French woman, Natalie Gueyne, whose parents spent the summer in the country and we were invited to stay at their pent house while they were away. We looked for the superintendent who had the key. We found him and my mom attempted to ask, in French, for the key. He looked at her like she was crazy. He acted like he knew nothing about it. I wonder if the word for key has a second meaning. I suggested we go to the apartment and knock on the door. My mom thought that would be a wasted effort but finally agreed. We knocked on the door and lo and behold a maid answered. My mom greeted her in French and told the maid that we were Lois and Jody Sack and we were here to stay for two weeks. The maid said, "non parlez." Again, we were stymied. For some reason, I decided to try Spanish and it worked. She was Spanish! We got in and she gave us her key. We were in Paris, with a great place to stay, and so relieved.

    We saw just about all the historical highlights and museums. In between, we discovered a huge park where we could run almost every morning. Bois de Boulogne reminded me of Fairmont Park in Philadelphia or Central Park in New York. We also took out a row boat and rowed around the lake. We even tried riding bikes. The bikes worked ok because I could focus on my mom's back wheel as she rode ahead. New things, like being able to ride a bike, in spite of blindness, were exciting to me.

    Totally French and fun, was my mom's friend Natalie. She invited us to her apartment and we discovered that, in addition to being a successful businesswoman, she was an artist. It was great being with someone who liked to practice her English.

My favorite museum was the Musee d'Orsay, a converted train station filled with French Impressionist paintings. I learned so much and it was a great experience. With my lousy vision, I was unable to see whole paintings, but I was able to see detail. My mom and I did have one moment of silliness at the Georges Pompidou Museum, tres moderne. We listened to a tour director describe a canvas painted totally black. He talked about rhythm and balance and wonderful contrast. All we saw was black. We started laughing and had to leave the tour.

At Sacre Coeur, we climbed many steps to see the view from the top. Even with my limited vision, it was worth the climb. Below, in the café area (I love side walk cafes), I had my picture drawn by an artist who wasn't French, but American! Afterwards we walked through Pigalle and I had an encounter. I walked smack into a pregnant French woman. She yelled at me and called me every name, some of which I understood. My mom said, in French, that I was blind and the French woman apologized. She couldn't have been nicer. I later said to my mom that the woman should be more careful where she is going, being pregnant and all. My mom just moaned.

I convinced my mom to go to London for the weekend. We stayed at my aunt's sister-in-law's house. She was one block from the train station and after a little walking around in circles we found it. Our hostess, Mary Gordon-Watson, who is so nice, gave us ideas for our two days. We took a hop-on, hop-off double decker bus and saw most of the highlights of London. The next day, we walked to Buckingham Palace and Westminster Abbey and Convent Gardens where we saw entertainers. I'm so glad that we got to see London and visit with Mary.

Chapter 19   Marathon Girl

Graduation from UVA was so much fun. For me, it was especially great because I had done well academically and I had a great bunch of friends. When I got back to Rosemont, Pennsylvania, I was still floating on a cloud of self respect, something I did not have much of a few years before. My fourth year at UVA was as wonderful as first year was awful. During first year, I can still remember calling my parents to beg to come home. My mom would say, "If you are sure, then come on home." Then I would have a decent few days and not mention going home for a week or so. The moral in this is: when you think life will never be fun again, give it another week.

I was a college graduate with a BA in English, living at home with no job prospects. Was I anxious? No. It was fun hanging around. It was relaxing to be with my family, dog, and old friends. The truth is, I was considering graduate school and was studying in a group to take my G Mats. Then I remembered Bobbi Cabrey, the sports editor of *The Main Line Times*, had once told me, while she was doing a story about my come back from my car accident, to call her anytime if I ever wanted to write about sports. I called and I got the job. Yeah! I was a sportswriter for a popular local newspaper. Bobbi thought I would be writing features and doing in-office interviews of coaches and athletes. I did these but I also got to go to games and write about the progression of those games. Sports' fans who stood near me were my best friends for a couple hours. I would keep saying, "What are they doing now." Most of the time, the informant was most helpful if his or her kid's team was winning.

Another accomplishment that summer after graduation was running in the Philadelphia Marathon. I trained with Liz McCue, a young mother of two (later three) children for whom I baby sat. She had already run five marathons. We trained most of the summer, running farther and farther each week. Finally, in November, 1995, the big day came. I was so nervous. I wrote about it for *The Main Line Times* (11-30-1995).

The headline was "Mission accomplished: Sack does Philly Marathon."

We had accomplished our goal—we ran the 1995 PhiladelphiaMarathon in under four hours! My official time was three hours and 45 minutes. After crossing the line, I felt faint and confused. The doctor in the first aid tent determined I was dehydrated and sent me to the hospital in an ambulance. The next couple hours I got fluids through tubes and lay in a hospital bed. But, it was worth it. Even though it was another reminder that my pituitary gland was still not functioning normally, regulating my need for fluids, it was also a reminder that I was not only as good a runner as I was before my car accident, I was better!

Chapter 20   Away Down South in Dixie

While I enjoyed working for *The Main Line Times*, especially working for Bobbi Cabrey, and writing about sports, I started to think that writing commercials and advertisements. Being a copy writer, would be better for me. For one thing, there is less dependence on travel and driving a car. Most copy writers work from an office. A friend of mine from high school was attending The Creative Circus, a graduate school in copy writing and design. He recommended it highly. I flew to Atlanta, Georgia, to check out my friend K.C., who was living there and to visit The Creative Circus. At the Circus, I met some of the nicest, most interesting teachers and students. I applied with some writing samples, including writing some ads, and to my great relief and joy, I was accepted.

K.C. invited me to share her apartment and I knew that would be great. Fortunately, K.C.'s apartment was quite close to the Creative Circus. I could take two buses or run along the highway. I knew right away I would love Atlanta. There were other transplants in our apartment complex that were about our age and K.C. had already rounded up a bunch of friends. The apartment complex had a pool, work-out room, areas where I could run, and just to be with K.C. was a guaranteed adventure.

K.C. (the K is for Kristin) is a 5', dark-complexioned and dark-haired, beautiful and intelligent person who thinks things out and is extremely considerate of others. I'm a 5' 9" blonde with a whatever will be will be attitude. We were a good balance and we admired each other.

The Creative Circus was a two-year course. Even though I was planning to be a copy writer, we all learned some design work which was helpful. I learned to be more creative, to think about new ways to present an idea or product. I tried to apply this to my personal life as well as my work life. The Circus hosted visiting teachers, successful ad men and women, who shared with us their formulas for thinking originally. One of those teachers was Nick Cohen, head of Mad Dogs and Englishmen, the hottest boutique ad agency in New York. When I graduated, I interned with Mad Dogs. Nick Cohen was one of the nicest persons I met in the business and he gave me a tremendous break.

Living in Atlanta occupied two of the best years of my life. I worked part-time as a sitter for babies and toddlers at The Atlanta Athletic Club, which was located within walking distance from the Creative Circus. As an employee, I could work out on the equipment and participate in special classes such as spinning and aerobics, as often as I wanted. But it was in my off time that I really had a blast. I was so lucky that one of my best friends from UVA, Ana Alain, and another, Bridget Burke, and several others lived there. They merged well with the friends K.C. had made and we all had so much fun.

Going for my runs (two to five miles) in Atlanta seemed pretty easy to me but my friends apparently rolled their eyes when I answered their questions of where I ran. My two favorite routes were to cross our street at the entrance and run down the busy road to an industrial park. The second route was along the highway. They may have been risky for a blind person, but running made me feel normal and I tried to be careful.

One mid-day, I came back from a run and felt dizzy. I sat on the front stairs and then passed out. Two of the building's maintenance men found me and brought me into my apartment. I thanked them and they made me promise to see a doctor. I saw an endocrinologist and learned that my pituitary gland was still not functioning 100% and that is why I got dehydrated, a problem from the accident I hoped would just go away.

The approaching Olympics was making Atlanta one of the most exciting cities. New people were in town to do special projects for the Olympics. Our neighbor, Lisa Montgomery, was a space designer who was asked to plan areas for Olympic hospitality centers for businesses and countries. She recruited several guys for the actual building of her masterpieces, including Jamie Whitehead from Cincinnati, Ohio. We were to become a couple. He was in Atlanta most of the time before the Olympics and visited Atlanta (and me) after the Olympics. Jamie was such a nice guy, always looking out for me, knowing when to hold my hand and when to speak directions as we walked. As I mentioned before, there are people who have a special ability to empathize with someone's disability, and he was one of those people.

 Jamie, who knows what might have been our future? We were no longer going together when I moved to New York City, but he told my mom that he hoped we might get back together. I'll always remember you, Jamie, with your white tee shirt that said, "Take an ax to tax." And who could forget our trips to hardware stores, you looooved hardware stores.

Chapter 21   "Just do it!"

The Olympics brought friends and relatives to Atlanta, some needing a place to stay. Among those that I went to events with was my mom. We went to rowing (hard to see), track and field (also hard to see) and the final night for women's gymnastics. Through Lisa and other friends, I got tickets for all those events except gymnastics. Having taken gymnastics for about eight years, I really wanted to see it, especially since the American team had a chance at gold. We thought for sure we could buy tickets from scalpers. No way. I felt so disappointed. I said to my mom, "Some way or other, I'm going to get in there." Well, we did. Let's just say my mom and I practiced a little drama for the ticket taker, arguing in front of her that I had brought the wrong tickets and the ticket taker finally felt sorry for us and let us in. It was worth the chance of being embarrassed. It was the final night when the Americans did win, thanks to Kerrie Strug who hurt her foot but went on to clinch the gold. After the event, we hurried back to my apartment to call my dad and brother to tell them to be sure to watch it on TV to the end (TV coverage was a couple hours after the events). Their first question was, "How did you get in?"

Almost everybody sometimes forgets where they parked their car. Well, my mom and I did worse than that. We lost our parking lot. After watching rowing, we had to board a bus to take us to our parking lot. But all the parking lots looked the same. We got off at the wrong one. It took us an hour to get another bus and find the right lot.

While all this was going on, my apartment mate, K.C., was falling in love. His name, is David Doerr and she met him through Villanova University friends. Before I knew it, they were planning to get married and I needed a new place to live. I was so happy for K.C. and David because they seemed just right for each other. My next roommate was a guy, Doug Loux, a member of our little group. Doug was special in so many ways, but the thing everyone knew about him as soon as they met him, was he had gone to the University of Tennessee and he loooved anything about Tennessee. Doug and I still communicate, and I am sorry Doug, I cannot influence football players in any way.

K.C.'s wedding was nothing but the best. And the best part for me was, I was a bridesmaid. There were showers and a great rehearsal dinner and the wedding was at the Basilica in Philadelphia and the reception at the Bellevue Hotel, also in Philadelphia. The bridal party and out-of-towners stayed at the

Bellevue. Everything was so elegant. K.C.'s parents are such good hosts, so very, very thoughtful. Along with the elegance, we still had much to laugh about. An old high school friend, Erica Stenstrom, was staying in the room with Jamie and me. I had gotten my hair done with the rest of the bridal party and then went to the room for a nap. The hair style was such that I could not lay on my back or my side without messing up my hair. When Jamie and Erica came in the room, they found me face down in the pillow in a deep sleep. For a moment, they thought I was dead.

Chapter 22 "I Love New York"

My next and final stop in my freight train of life was New York City. I was offered an internship (paid) at Mad Dogs and Englishmen, the best possible place for me. Neil Cohen said he liked my work and saw great potential. Was I afraid to move to such a huge, confusing city? Yes and no. I wanted to be there. It's where the action is. It is the center of the advertising business. It was helpful for a blind person to live in New York with walk lights on every corner and an endless supply of busses, subways, trains and taxi cabs. The only thing that worried me was: could I make it as a copy writer? I still wanted to be perceived as normal and not given special treatment because I was blind.

I moved into the apartment of my University of Virginia roommate Karen Pries. She had a studio next to The Javits Center, in the Chelsea section at 39th Street. It was tiny, but she worked nights as a nurse and I worked days, so we rarely got in each other's way. Karen never hesitated to offer me a place to stay when I told her I was coming to New York. She was, is, such a good friend. I stayed there for about six months. Then, through a friend at Mad Dogs, I heard that a friend of his was looking for someone to share his rent. I couldn't stay with Karen forever; there just wasn't room, so I went to see the other apartment, in the Gramercy section at East 16 Street. From here, I could walk to work. I moved in with my new apartment mate, Rob Lovett, who was working in international finance. It was a good move; we got along great.

Work turned out to be very competitive but extremely educational and rewarding. The office was laid back, with the copy writers arriving in mid morning and staying late. Neil Cohen's style was to do a great job for clients where we could be very creative and off the wall. He was known to have turned down a famous, huge bank that asked him to pitch.

I enjoyed most everyone in our office, especially Ulrika Welender, a girl my age from Sweden who was also an intern. Ulrika had a night job as a waitress at one of the most "in" places in New York City. She got me into the back room where the celebrities go. It was great bringing other friends there.

My high school friend, Sabrina Waltheim, who lived in New York, once said to me: "You either love New York right away or you don't love it, ever." I loved it right away. I may have had New York in my brain for years. When I was 11 years old, my floor exercise for gymnastics was to the song, "New York,

New York," originally sung by Frank Sinatra. My mom, brought up in New Rochelle, New York, had talked about the year she worked in Manhattan and had so much fun. It just seemed so right for someone who could never drive a car and was ambitious about her career, and, bottom line, loved excitement.

Anti-New Yorkers have been known to accuse New Yorkers of being unfriendly, ruthless, unsympathetic and dishonest. When I hear this, I think of an incident that happened to me at the LaGuardia Airport. I was leaving New York for a weekend in Atlanta. I got to the airport early, so I went for a snack at one of the airport concessions. Then I went through security. As I approached the gate waiting area, I noticed my wallet was missing from my backpack. I panicked and went to find a security guard. He said in a calm and not too sympathetic voice, "Where did you last use it?" I told him I had a snack but I didn't notice the name of the concession. I told him my plane was boarding but I would go back to security and see if it was there (this was in 1998, before you needed to show a picture I.D.). The security folks acted a bit hurt that anyone would lose anything in their province and I double panicked. I was sure if I had left it at the concession, someone would have taken it by now. Fortunately, I had my ticket for the plane. I would have to go to

Atlanta where my friend, Ana, was picking me up at the airport. I couldn't go home to my apartment because I had no bus or cab money. I was lucky the plane hadn't taken off and I got to the gate just in time. As I was showing my ticket to the attendant, I felt someone nudging my shoulder and heard him say, out of breath, "Miss, I found your wallet. Here it is." It was the unsympathetic-looking security guard. He had been searching for it and I never thought to ask him where he found it. I was so happy I hugged him and thanked him so much. And that's my example of a friendly, sympathetic and honest New Yorker.

Another reason for being enchanted with New Yorkers is the variety of cultures, accents, and genders. Ulrika and I belonged to the same gym, so sometimes we worked out together during lunch. One of our favorite classes was spinning (stationary bike riding with a leader who told you to add or take away pressure making it harder or easier to pedal). One of the spin meisters was a transvestite. The leaders are supposed to spend most of the time on their bikes, telling us what to do and urging us on. This leader never got on her bike except in the beginning. She walked (swished) around yelling at us if she thought we were cheating on the pressure. I will say, we got a good workout.

One time, after my internship ended (one year), I was scheduled to have two interviews for a copy writing job in one afternoon. I finished the first and was running a little late for the second. I thought I knew the way so I was walking much faster than I usually do. I was dressed at my best, in a new brown pants suit and high heels. Well, I was passing someone and I tripped on the short wire fence the City puts around fledgling trees. I went down hard, ripped my pants at the knees and scraped my hands. An older, ethnic woman, with a realllll New York accent reached down to help me up and said, "Oh my God! Look at you! You're bleeding: You tripped and look at you. Are you all right? You poor thing." By then, a small group of people had gathered around to see what was going on. After brushing me off and hugging me and patting my face and what else, this kind and motherly woman turned to the people watching and said, "They got to get rid of these fucking trees!" Only in New York!

I went on to the interview and my excuse for being late was obviously "an accident." I think telling the interviewer the story allowed him to get to know me a little too well. But he said he would call me and perhaps he did.

Running in New York is a challenge, blind or sighted. I liked going new ways, always looking for the perfect route. To rationalize my clumsiness, I would think, "If people would only walk straight and not cut left and right; if skate boarders, roller-bladders, bike riders, mothers with strollers and baby carriages, other runners, and most of all, wheel chair users would please stay out of my way (just kidding), there would be less cursing and yelling from both colliding parties. My 20 per cent of vision in the one "good" eye is usually focused on the sidewalk about five yards ahead or "walk" lights up high—my sight did not take in extraneous equipment. Oh yes, there's dogs. I have plowed into little and big ones, and it has never been friendly. Rollie, my dog, learned early to get out of the way when I approached unless I was saying his name.

After I died, my apartment mate, Rob, was asked about me by Kay Raftery of the *Philadelphia Inquirer*. He kindly spoke about my running and not about the people and objects I bumped into along the way. He said, "She came to New York and only had limited sight, so every day was a risk. But she'd go running every day and rarely did she come back without another scrape on her knees from tripping on cracks or falling, but she'd get up the next day and go out again. I never met anyone like her."

The word is that I interned longer than anyone else at Mad Dogs. It was a great year. When I left, the staff had a going-away party for me. They kidded me about tripping on dogs (staff members often brought their dogs to work). Also on the "watch out, here comes Jody" list was one particular waste basket. Neil Cohen gave me a broom and I was allowed to bash the waste basket until it could no longer perform its duty.

It seemed like where ever I went, University of Virginia, Atlanta, or New York, there were always some friends from Radnor High School to make my life more comfortable. There was Sabrina, one of the smartest and prettiest and most talented girls I have ever known. Another New York friend was Jen Renzi, who was also brilliant (went to Yale and then NYU) and beautiful and an outstanding swimmer for RadnoThey were always there for me, to call on the phone or go places with.

Another friend, Suzanne Delenge, did not go to my high school but I knew her from swimming. She moved to New York and loved it as I did. She says she'll never forget the time she invited me over for the Super Bowl. It was a mild January day and I decided to run through Central Park to her apartment near Columbus Avenue. The Super Bowl had started and I was not there. The phone rang and it was me. I told her I was lost and what number street I was on and she said, "Jody, you missed the turn, you are in Harlem." I finally made it there before the half.

Chapter 23   One Fatal Misstep

In May, 1998, I was hit by a school bus while running. I had learned to time the walk lights precisely so that I could still cross a street after walk was over, before the traffic was supposed to advance. I approached a corner on First Avenue and sprinted, while listening to music from my "head phones" (what was I thinking?). I was in a very confident mood when I went "bang" into the mirror that projects way out from the bus from the driver's side. You could say, it was I who hit the bus. It knocked me down and out. An ambulance took me to Beth Israel Medical Center, practically across the street from my apartment building. There was no apparent damage except a massive, swollen, black eye...my good eye.

Well, I certainly created a reaction when people saw me. It was a combination of "poor girl" to "Ugh, what a mess." It wasn't pretty. But that didn't stop me from going on a University of Virginia alumni boat trip around Manhattan that evening. Plans had been made with Karen and we had already paid. Karen took one look at me and suggested I stay home but of course I did not. To me, the black eye was just another of life's ordinary hard knocks.

By mid June, the swelling and blackness had receded about half way. I figured I looked almost normal enough to continue my job interviews. I had a good resume and the experience of interning for an agency with a great reputation for creativity. I was optimistic. But, for the first time in a long time, I was also feeling less confident about my getting around because of the bus collision. For the first time in New York I was, I hate to admit it, scared.

My interviews went well, especially at Mezzina, Brown where they offered me a free-lance opportunity. I was so happy. This meant I would be working full time probably but I would not be on the payroll and receive benefits right away. This is the way an ad agency usually starts a new copy writer.

I called my parents to tell them I had a job and I was coming home for a few days. I wanted to see my eye doctor, Madeleine Ewing, because I was worried that I hadn't gotten back a full 20% of vision in my seeing eye since my accident with the bus.

My mom, dad, and I had fun when I was home. We rode around in my mom's new (used) SAAB convertible which I had encouraged her to buy before she gets too old. Dr. Ewing assured me that I had not lost any more vision in my good eye. Whew! And I made a rather mature decision that I never could have made years ago. I was going to accept my blindness and not be so risky in my life style. We went to the store on Walnut Street in Philadelphia that sells things that help blind people. I bought a new white cane with a red tip...the official cane for people trained to walk with it. I had received training years ago but was too embarrassed to use it. Now I was ready. Like everyone says, you have to have your schist in New York and my schist was a long, red and white stick.

I wanted to get back to New York that Friday, June 27, for several reasons, including going to a rooftop cookout in the East Village, given by some friends. I said "good-bye" to my mom at 30th Street Station, Philadelphia. I was back to New York in time to go for a run and call my brother who wasn't home when I had visited this weekend.

I walked to the apartment in the East Village with Rob, my apartment mate, and a few of our friends. I didn't bring my new cane because I had people with me. I was really looking forward to a picnic on a roof, a very New York thing to do. The party was fun, as expected. Time flew, and before we knew it, it was after midnight and we were cleaning up, planning to stop off at a favorite bar on the way home.

We had to leave the roof by fire escape. I was the last to go except for a sister of one of the guys hosting the party. The next thing I knew, I heard her screaming. She was hysterical for a long time, although I only heard her for a few seconds as I was falling down four stories.

The Philadelphia Inquirer, July 1, 1998, ran the following headline on page one: "A tragic misstep ends a life of hope and courage."

The girl left on the roof told police that I reached for the railing of the fire escape as I stepped closer to the edge of the roof. I grabbed air, stepped into air, and fell over the side, landing four stories below. My injuries were fatal, I had landed on the back of my head. Rob gave me artificial respiration but he couldn't revive me.

For my friends who may suspect a presence of drugs and alcohol, the New York City coroner said they found no evidence that drugs or alcohol played a part in my death. They blamed it on my lack of depth perception.

When I fell those four stories off that roof top, I didn't make a sound. I was too busy thinking what my mom, dad, and brother were going to say and watching my last eight years pass before me. Those eight years were the best and worst of my 25 years. They started bad with flipping my car and ended worse with my fall from a roof, but in-between, it was one extraordinary adventure after another.

I am no longer a part of this world. I'm like an outsider looking in. My thoughts are becoming clear.

Whether your life is long or short, it is quality that counts. Try to love your family and tell them. Maintain good friends. Set goals. Be as kind, honest and brave as you can be. And, if you believe in God, as I do, He is there to comfort you.

Newspaper Quotes of the Fatal Misstep

Bobbi Cabrey, sports editor at the *Main Line Times*, wrote a beautiful, final story about Jody. The headline was "Jody's gift; a better view of the world." She said, "Maybe these last eight years [since the car accident] were really a gift from God, a special exemption."

A friend of Jody's, Sabrina Walheim, was interviewed by Kay Rafferty of *The Philadelphia Inquirer*. Sabrina said, "Jody taught me how to be brave and defy the small aggravations in life and my greatest regret is that I won't have the opportunity to learn more from her. Jody saw possibilities instead of problems."

Bobbi Cabrey concluded: "Jody did not live her life to inspire. She was just being herself."

Addendum
Eulogy at Bryn Mawr Presbyterian Church
By T.J Sack (brother of Jody)

"Today, we are here to celebrate the life of my sister, Jody Lynn Sack. In order to do this, I figured I would let you all hear what Jody has accomplished in her short but spirited and wonderful life. In high school, Jody was mostly recognized for sports, as she excelled in swimming, lacrosse, and cross country. But most people do not remember the fact that she was a scholar, being involved in the National Honor Society. She also participated in many service clubs, such as a member of the Radnor High School Service Board, vice president of the Interact Service Club, president of the Youth Representative Board at Bryn Mawr Presbyterian Church, a Red Cross member, a member of Surrey Club for seniors and a member of Trevor's Campaign, which feeds the homeless.

Then, as most of you already know, Jody was in a near fatal car accident, which was only a setback for Jody to keep on living. It reminds me of a recent song that Jody liked to relate to herself, by the group Chumbawumba. The song's theme is "I Get Knocked Down, But I Get Up Again. They're Never Going to Keep Me Down."

And Jody was definitely knocked down in her accident. A week after her accident, while she was in the hospital at The Medical College of Pennsylvania, I remember my family and I were very excited when Jody was able to only squeeze our hands when we asked her to. And even after two months, she was still generally confined to a wheel chair, but they were never going to keep her down.

About four months after her accident, Jody was at Villanova University for one semester of classes and then she was off to the University of Virginia. Most individuals go through college not doing much of anything but concentrating on their studies and social lives, and Jody, being legally blind, that was what most of us expected. Not Jody however. She was a member of the Virginia Women's Crew Team for four years, on the committee for the independence for students with disabilities, and a writer for the UVA newspaper, yearbook, and a student advocate newsletter. Even in the summers between semesters at UVA, Jody worked hard as she possibly could. Jody worked at WCAU-TV with Herb Denenberg; Smith Barney: the mail room of the *Suburban and Wayne Times*, as a telemarketing representative, a writer for the local section of *the Philadelphia Inquirer*, and a few stints at Club La Maison. She certainly kept busy.

Remarkably, after four years of listening to talking books for her textbooks, she graduated with a BA in English from the University of Virginia in 1995. From there she went to work at the *Main Line Times* under Bobbi Cabrey, sports editor, and on the side, trained for a marathon with Liz McCue, our neighborhood friend. When she eventually ran in the marathon, she finished in three hours and forty-five minutes, averaging under a nine-minute mile. If you can remember, the only thing that she could do about five years earlier was squeeze her family's hands, and five years later she ran an impressive marathon.

From here, Jody just kept on running all the way down to Atlanta. She enrolled in an advertising school called the Creative Circus, where she majored in copy writing. Throughout this whole time, she worked at a fitness club in the daycare section, keeping busy as usual. She went to Atlanta knowing only a few people, but came out with a ton of close friends, really creating a life for herself. Soon after her graduation from advertising school, she moved onto the big city, New York. She interned at a successful ad agency called Mad Dogs and Englishmen for a year and was ready to start a new job this week. She had made it through the toughest times and seemed to be at the pinnacle of her happiness and success since the time of her car accident. Jody Lynn Sack died a happy and successful woman.

All these things Jody accomplished were outstanding, always moving on, always doing better than before. But these do not fully represent Jody. They don't show the little things that we would all see every day, like her smile, kindness, humor, courage, and determination. She always kept on moving, never letting anything keep her down. Whether she was running that extra mile or reaching out to meet a new friend, she did it, even though it was a little harder for her than it would be for us. A friend of the family, Andy Thompson, dropped off a quote this week because he felt it was a true representation of Jody and it really is. It reads:

> "A person can make himself happy or miserable regard-less of what is happening on the outside, just by changing the context of consciousness.
> We all know individuals who can transform hopeless situations into challenges to be overcome just through the force of their personalities. This ability to persevere despite obstacles and set-

backs is the quality people most admire in others and justly so. It is probably the most important trait not only for succeeding in life, but enjoying it as well."

In ending, Jody was a spirited and courageous person from whom we all can learn. She definitely did not take the precious moments of life for granted. Her devotion to her friends, her family and herself made her short life really one worth living. So let's remember her life in celebration, not despair, as that is what Jody would want us to do.

Made in the USA
Lexington, KY
26 December 2014